Also by Benjamín Naka-Hasebe Kingsley

Colonize Me
Not Your Mama's Melting Pot

DĒMOS

AN AMERICAN MULTITUDE

BENJAMÍN NAKA-HASEBE KINGSLEY

MILKWEED EDITIONS

Published 2021 by Milkweed Editions
Printed in XXX
Cover design by Mary Austin Speaker
Cover art by Salman Khoshroo
21 22 23 24 25   5 4 3 2 1
First Edition

Milkweed Editions, an independent nonprofit publisher, gratefully acknowledges sustaining support from the Alan B. Slifka Foundation and its president, Riva Ariella Ritvo-Slifka; the Ballard Spahr Foundation; *Copper Nickel*; the McKnight Foundation; the National Endowment for the Arts; the National Poetry Series; the Target Foundation; and other generous contributions from foundations, corporations, and individuals. Also, this activity is made possible by the voters of Minnesota through a Minnesota State Arts Board Operating Support grant, thanks to a legislative appropriation from the arts and cultural heritage fund. For a full listing of Milkweed Editions supporters, please visit milkweed.org.

Library of Congress Cataloging-in-Publication Data

Last, first.
Title : subtitle / by author.
p. cm.
ISBN 1-57131-___-__
ISBN 978-57131_-__-_
I. Title
XXxxxx.xxxXxx 1994
xxx'.xx—dc20xx-xxxxx
CIP

Milkweed Editions is committed to ecological stewardship. We strive to align our book production practices with this principle, and to reduce the impact of our operations in the environment. We are a member of the Green Press Initiative, a nonprofit coalition of publishers, manufacturers, and authors working to protect the world's endangered forests and conserve natural resources. *Dēmos* was printed on acid-free _____% postconsumer-waste paper by _____.

In Memory of Timmy

Acknowledgments

Un fuerte abrazo to the anthologies and journals in which many of these pieces appeared, sometimes in earlier forms:

Anthology of Appalachian Writers, Vol. XII

The BreakBeat Poets Anthology, Vol. 4: LatiNEXT

Contemporary Chicanx Writers Anthology

Genre: Urban Arts' House Anthology

Native Voices: Honoring Indigenous Poetry Anthology

Poetry Daily

Proud to Be: Writing by American Warriors Anthology, Volume 8

Rewilding: Anthology of Poems for the Environment

Verse Daily

American Indian Culture and Research Journal

The Asian American Literary Review

Blackbird

Boston Review

Colorado Review

Ecotone

FIELD

Fourth Genre

The Georgia Review

Gulf Coast

Image

International Journal of Indigenous Literature

the minnesota review

Missouri Review

New England Review

The Paris–American

Poetry

Poetry Northwest

Puerto del Sol

Rattle

Southern Indiana Review

Tin House

Waxwing

West Branch

Contents

but man is born to trouble
as the sparks fly upward

−ELIPHAZ

4,000 YEARS AGO (CIRCA 2070 B.C.)

Dēmos:

1. "of the people." Free, self-governing citizens
2. "assembly," "crowd," or "public congress." Originally denoted a "divided portion" but came to focus upon the fellowship of citizens, as those who belong, united.

American Multitude

from the languages of my Haudenosaunee: Onondaga Nation

      as every thing begins   with the heart   beat of horses

a tribe   the thudded color   of all creation

      my people gather   brindle   as if the night

were drizzled long   across their backs   she

      of sickle sword   of tendon & tusk   he

who wields the oxgoad   fresh   jawbone

      from a filly   in heat   they

who buck   the binary   tekeni Jonijüra

      two-Spirited   a young soul miracles   how many?

ghosts can fit inside   my people   gather brindle

      as if the night were not   yet gelded   my people

gather   as if the night   were a suckling

      for the saber-toothed   drum   the whistle of pipes

crescentic & long   hatchet my people   gather as

      if the night   were   only a splintered thing

bent   about   the glory

      of our now   dawning   home.

———

Nantucket Sleighride

When you harpoon a whale, it bucks harder than a freight train
off rails. It dives down deep as it can go, and takes your boat
with it—fast—and that's the "sleigh ride": that last fighting gasp
of leviathan through the sea.

—BROWNING TYLER, GRANDSON OF A NANTUCKET WHALER, 81YRS OLD

You know the whale metaphor. You know all about
the beaten horse. Write this off as just another
dead animal poem. Or, dying, know that my people
weren't neatly arked by America two by two, white boys named
Noah harpooned our asses, by the tens, by the thousands,
collared our necks with barbs and slugged lead
into our heads when we bucked, they dove in after
our oil and the good fat of our plains, from Sea to Shining
Sea. Now here we all are, a tangle of corpses
together we crabs in a clawed bucket list:
cross off every otherkind and colony—colonize
the crevice between my brown lungs, cremate me
in ashy anonymity before
I surface, I breathe, I war.

America Our Punnett;
Square Now? Square It.

WWhite skin ; BBlue eyes
*For every Male
Penobscot Indian above
the Age of Twelve Years,
that shall be taken and
brought to Boston, Fifty
Pounds…. For every* "

WWhite skin ; BBlue eyes
*SCALP of a Male
Penobscot Indian above
the Age aforesaid,
brought in as Evidence
of their being killed
as aforesaid, Forty
Pounds…. For every* "
Female

WWhite skin ; BBlue eyes
*Penobscot Indian taken
and brought in as
aforesaid, and for every
Male Indian Prisoner
under the Age of Twelve
Years, taken and brought* "

RRed skin ; BBrown eyes
BBlue river ; CClear sky

Rred skin ; Bbrown eyes
Bblue river ; Cclear sky

black field ; our genocide
but we are alive ; I am alive

WWhite skin ; BBlue eyes
*Twenty-five Pounds….
For every SCALP of
such Female Indian or
Male Indian under the
Age of Twelve Years,
that shall be killed and
brought in* "

rred skin ; bbrown eyes
bblue river ; cclear sky

light skin ; heavy eyes
yellow river ; red sky

---

n By His Honour, Spencer Phips Lieutenant-Governor and Commander in Chief, in and over His Majesty's Province of the Massachusetts-Bay in New-England

6

An Old Song, a Frog's Song

> There once was a giant kci-coqols, a bullfrog
> big as a hill. He made love to The Lake
> and Her children were born of land and water, many
> as the pebbles on Her hips, the waist of Her shoreline.
> Now, when The Lake is poisoned and Her spirit
> will cause people harm, Her children are the first
> to tell us. They are the first to die.*

Sing long   on America   as One
body   but many parts   of The Lake
says   great   grandmother

Sing long   on all the tribes   who *were*
and   drank from Her   once-blue lips
knelt   to wash   a child's hair
long black   to   long black
who are now *not*   but   a ghosted edge
mislaid names   Red   how many
of kci-coqols'   kin   must have drown
in our carnage   bellied-up   Native in Her body
where white man's   hands   were washed
blood red   to lake blue then   white again
says   great   grandmother

Sing long   on how many more   deaths
a flood   of broken duck necks   still
gulp for one last   melody   Trees gorged
with yellow-bodied   canaries   choke
on the cancer   of men's   love
for coal for oil for the   glacier's   hot
melting   in the chandelier   of a whisky glass
says   great   grandmother

Sing long   on the price   of blood
of black   soil   of treasure
if men could   silo sunlight   peddle
its glisten above   Her blue   body
they would   oh they   would
says   great   grandmother

Listen   for the old   song
for   the shore   song
for   the frog   song Listen
for   Her children's   one small song

Then   sing
with your   whole   body
    sing
for all   who are   to come
    sing
says   great   grandmother
    sing

American Rust

Buried   palm to palm   beneath floorboards
trapped residue   of her forefather's will   small
cowhide gloves   burnt orange   well-battered

gloves so small   she knows   she could slip
inside them   how her hands will   reek
of sheet metal   the upriver   trout

for days   her fins   flail against a greasy fate below
the yellowed   rocks of her fingernails   oil squirms
reminding her   for years of   factory men

weekend walks   to the laundromat   tangled trash bags
bursting with work   clothes   the stained glint
of beer   glasses clacked   with weekday husbands

caught in their sloshing   gait of hunger   patina of bootfall
each wade   slow   home in *hammy down*
pickups   loosened tool belts   each exhale then hard won

now left to her   mechanic's daughter   a better life
in her studio   the corner kiln fires   each day's work uneven
one armful of clay dried   to the bone   others wet

everlasting some of her   work   will never dry
a small rebellion   against the modern   mouth of automation
humanity whirring   on the primacy   of a future tense

her hands are wet   with the glaze   of decades
undying   memories overworked   so painstakingly
greased in American oil   they never truly   rust

In the Coffin Meant for Chief Little Horse, Archeologists Instead Find Two Others

Two right hip bones—
all that remains
of three Native boys
buried in one coffin
1,892 miles away
from their Arapaho
Wind River tribe,
their rightful home.

"There were hundreds
of *transplants* to Carlisle:
your grandfather's Indian
Industrial School," says my mother,
timidly, as if the White Man
will break into this kitchen and take
the two of us Indians, too.

I think, maybe—maybe
my grandfather knew
these two boys, desired
to feel the harsh consonants
of their English names on the bed
of his Haudenosaunee tongue. Maybe he braided
their wolf spider hair. Maybe they spoke
of entering death together
beneath Pennsylvania pines:

because I know that cemetery—
exactness of yellowed headstones, next
to the Soldier's Lot, and because
I have sat under the girth of quaking
aspens, their honeyed heads,
yellow combs, leafs of long hair,
and because I have raked my forearms

with tines of confused adolescence,
picked the balk of brown skin
from beneath my fingernails, and because
I have understood the eulogy,
the saber rattling, the war cry
of European English
paper WASPs, yellow jackets
in frenzied debate
just above my left ear:

In whose home will we build our next nest?
In whose home will we build our next nest?
In whose home will we build our next nest?

In whose home will we build our next nest?
In whose home will we build our next nest?
In whose home will we build our next nest?

In whose home will we build our next nest?
In whose home will we build our next nest?
In whose home will we build our next nest?

Sons of Cain: Hunting a Ridge between Lockwood and Sizerville State Park

"Fire," hisses my Paw   in full regalia
us two orange bulbs   of florescent death
hunkering   among red oak and switches
of witch hazel.   I press the .243
tighter   against my right shoulder.
The eyepiece on its scope   coring
my wide white eye   juicing it down
my soft sun browned   cheeks so full
of violence   and the lunch of Vienna
sausages   I'd upchucked secretly
behind sweet birch   or maybe shagbark?
I've never   been good
at IDing trees.   Paw's left eye fires
from me to the doe   from me to the doe
stomach acid still tugging   on the trigger
of my throat.   *Sweet Jesus*
He's thinking so loud   I can hear the brattling
of slurs   through my earplugs.
Fire, you little pussy.   *Your skin softer*
than split sausage?   He'll chaw me
between them ivory   dentures. He'll
turn   my hide inside out
surer   than any sure thing.
I take stock   of the brown doe her
bare head   and pregnant belly
my crosshairs bobbing   between exposed
foreleg and shoulder.   If
if I breathe   life
into   a single bullet
dormant now   in the chamber
hammer and pin   it will shatter
her   lungs
it will powder us   in two
our most   basic parts.

How to Clean a Boy

Triple check the joist   hooked
from your garage   ceiling
is rated for at least   97 pounds.

Spear his calves   with T-hanger
with gambrel & let   the rusty hitch
of your truck   do the hard work

pulling cord taut   till he's vertical
as Christ   on a 2x4. Pray
for the palms   preparing supper. Your

very own. Slit   the olive skin
around his sissyboy   ankles. &
remember   the key to good meat

is separation   from its fur.
Grind your skinning   knife
sharper   than obsidian.

Blade incisions   precise at 10
& 2 & steer   his hide down
toward the slop   bucket

brim red   with offal. Keep
going or   his body might warm
into another kind   of kneejerk

wriggling   like an unfrozen fish
tossed silvery   in a pond thawed of
guilt & comatose   motion.

Not a kindness.   Wash him
gently   with a hose. Know deep
un-downed   he is only meat & bones.

Wipe   the blood
first   from your floors,
second   your conscience.

Below Our Tree, Stands

an entire season   of velvet   horns wade

through turquoise   this pond   overrun with lily

pads of forty-four   hooves kicking   up bottom silt

algae splashed   across the rudder   of eleven whitetails

antlered enormous   their rust-   rinsed coats

sail   as floating oaks   beginning life

The rifle   clap   echo's

an entire season   of velvet   horns lurch

through turquoise   this pond   overrun with ruby

pads of forty   hooves kicking   up bottom silt

algae splashed   across the rudder   of ten whitetails

antlered enormous   one rust-   rinsed coat

sinks   as a razed oak another's   life just beginning

In One Small Bedroom, My Mother's Antlers

men wind
their hands
so tight
'round
my mother's
antlers
their crackle
is fresh
branch snap
is bough
to break
the arrow
shaft

lips of
brown bark
peeled back
a toothy
finish
each wipes
the blood
of his palms
off
on the back
of her
skull
it's not long
now
till
men will squeeze
her bones so
tight those bones
they'll clatter
milky

worn dice
unclogged
from the cofferdam
of her throat
across my bedroom
floorboards
then won't
the rest
of our life
be just
one fucking
gamble.

"Get Out of the Goddamn Car,"

says my father   and I'm leaping
out onto the highway pavement   the road
is not a spilled ribbon   of bow-tied asphalt not
the powdered rib   cage of likely-beaten
boys it is just   bumfuck
concrete.   I ragdoll
through God's   unpaved
underbelly His surfacing   pebble-pocked lesions
curl my hands   against a guardian angel
who never   never came alive for me
in faith I stretch   myself long across traffic
lane after unending lane   as if
there is a mother's minivan   who will take me
far from the floodgates   of heaven
buoy me to safety   restart my world with a rainbow
like Noah's magic boat never   dreamt it could.

Out My Apartment Window, West Baltimore: August, 2 A.M.

I spread the blinds
with sleepy fingers:

Three boys
and a lookout fourth
none old enough
to drive the car
they're prowling
around:

My Marlboro
-colored sedan,
a Benz twenty-something
years old & seated
atop bald wheels
soggy under the weight
of rain & faded
parking lot
lights:

I think more
& more
she's the one
thing my father left me
I've ever really used.
It's a hell:

Of a time
they're having.
Attempt after:

Attempt
to pry the ornament
from hood, paint-peeled

& chipped enough
to reveal the gray
of stone beneath:

Five minutes
of sneakers mounted
on her grill & a flurry
of whimpering tugs
a real sword in the stone
scenario:

I lay back down
in bed and hope
within an anvil of heart
that one boy will
free the silver:

And to him
it will be
Excalibur:

And he will
brandish the star
the ornament the sword
long as a boy can:

Understand
there is no
outstretched arm. No
Lady hidden in crystal-misted Lake.
Every old white wizard
would see you burned
alive. Here no Merlin
will shoulder the spell
of all your weight:

With your own arm
you cut.
With your own arm
you take:

Here
we get after
our own.
From the gray
of stones we pry
we pull each jewel
of light. Here
we forge
our own:

Bodies laid
long
upon the anvil
of this street.

A Punnett Square *Long Since Made and Frequently Renewed*

WWhite skin   ;   BBlue eyes   ;   WWhite skin   ;   BBlue eyes

For every Male Penobscot Indian above the Age of Twelve Years,
that shall be taken and brought to Boston, Fifty Pounds…. For every

Rred skin   ;   bbrown eyes   ;   rred skin   ;   Bbrown eyes

SCALP of a Male Penobscot Indian above the Age aforesaid, brought in
as Evidence of their being killed as aforesaid, Forty Pounds…. For every Female

Rred skin   ;   BBrown eyes   ;   llight skin   ;   Hheavy eyes

Penobscot Indian taken and brought in as aforesaid, and for every Male Indian
Prisoner under the Age of Twelve Years, taken and brought in as aforesaid,

yyellow river   ;   Rred sky   ;   BBlack field   ;   our genocide

Twenty-five Pounds…. For every SCALP of such Female Indian or Male Indian
under the Age of Twelve Years, that shall be killed and brought in n[n]

they were alive   ;   they were alive   ;   they were alive   ;   i am alive

---

[n] By His Honour, Spencer Phips
Lieutenant-Governor and Commander in Chief,
in and over His Majesty's Province
of the Massachusetts-Bay in New-England
where *the Tribe of Penobscot Indians have repeatedly*
in a perfidious Manner acted contrary
to their solumn Submission unto His Majesty
long since made and frequently renewed

Run Home, Boy: 2nd Street   Harrisburg PA   Summertime '17

Bullshit   watch your sister   be arrested
for daring   to dance   her jay-stunting
across the street   be next   to her but say
nothing   because this ain't   Footloose
and you will   always be   a coward
instead just be   thankful   for iphones
filming   for women   with stronger
forearms   for men   with bigger
voices   think instead about   your next
drink   don't be   thinking
about   every other   time
you were   not   brave
don't be   thinking   *I am a teacher*
sometimes   I even smile   at cops
I can win   this one over   with kind reason
he is bald   white   short
his uniform   has come   untucked
be close   enough   to see cliché
sweat   on his upper lip   be brave
be brave   you think   about anything but
boot scrape   baton clatter   police-grade
mace   your own knee's   crunch
against storefront   signpost   stumbling away
I could be   blind   what if I am
blind   forever   you think
why am I   mouthing   *Excuse me, Sir?*

Home/boy

On August 5th I was maced in the face by two cops.
I was visiting my hometown for the first time
in years. I was Center City with some old friends from elementary,
middle, and high school. A young woman, smaller than five foot, was being
arrested by over a dozen cops. I guess I got too close
to *the other.*

When my friends asked the cops why
mace me in the face—it was a homecoming celebration—
an officer said: "This ain't no hometown
for that homeboy." Then
they laughed.

• Essay transcribed by i: *witness*
that guy "maced directly in the face"

Exercise an anonymous Exegesis: Why did it take the baker's dozen
to subdue Paola Flores-Gonzalez, 18 years old?

August 5th   2nd Street   Harrisburg, PA

PennLive Headline: LOCAL COPS USE MACE   TO CONTROL

"UNCOOPERATIVE AND AGGRESSIVE"   CROWD

WHILE MAKING ARREST

Comments section with i's line break:

an/ad/vocate:
> immigration status needs / questioned
> when criminal / activity is / involved, unless
> she spoke / American / dialect English.

spar/hawk2002:
> If / the police would've / had updated riot gear
> like they've been / asking / for, they would've had more
> options / at their disposal, such / as nets, bean bag
> shotgun bullets, tasers. All of them would / hurt / like crazy

cost/ello:
> Did they call / ICE?

Still/Nun/yabiznes:
> I love the stupidity / of some complaining
> that the police didn't need / to use mace…
> guess / they should have given / hugs and butterfly kisses

unROOly:
> Good !! /!/ !! / I hope it burned like / heck.

Rangerider:
> Thank you / officers / for your fine work. It's a shame
> there are some in the city / who would try / to interfere
> in your great work and make good work / look
> bad. Don't / forget / to replenish your mace
> for the next bunch / of immigrants!

mburgsb:
> Another illegal / taking / up taxpayer / resources

dratsablive:

> From an eye / witness / who / was right there where / it happened:
> "There was no unruly crowd, the cops were blocking the sidewalk,
> which led to the sidewalk getting congested with pedestrians
> trying to walk around. Most of the 'crowd' didn't know
> or care what was going on. The cops literally only said 'move'
> 3 times, but gave nobody time to / move / before they maced
> a guy directly in the face, then the rest of the people trying to get around."

second1st (@dratsablive):

> I know that guy, he was the same / eye / witness
> that told me / Michael Brown / was / on his knees
> with his hands up / when that cop / shot / him.

"Write About Being Tri-racial," Says that Guy from Workshop

I was born what I am in ash   under cigarette flick

bellied beneath PA   roadside diner bulbs

I was born cooking   leftover ingredients

a little of this a little   of half of a half I was

born scraps   stirred see-through

in Pyrex   I was born dribbled

from God's measuring   cracked lip I was

born runny   eggs in a black skillet

though I was not yellow enough   for yolk

not black enough to be burnt   not even brown

enough to be sizzle-whispered   all the way

I was born trying to pass   off the problem

of not being born a breakfast food at all   my hatred of

egg whites the worst   their glueyness stuck in the front

of my throat   in the consonants of my Captors

you shake your head   you say, *Race is not extended*

food metaphor I say, *What   if it's true*

I was born in the morning   on a cold bed

of coffee grounds   crawling on egg shells I say,

You tell me how I was born   what I am

From Our Childhood Home / Now
Deserted / My Brother Takes
Nothing / Save One
Metal Cap / of Momma's
Moonshine Brew / He
Beats / that Tambourine
in Time / Against
Kitchen Table / Hollers
One Last Song / for the Floorboards
Us Ghosts:

Texaco station gas / and them canopied

lights / Only damn / thing   keep this small

town / bright / Daddy see me come   / home /

say it's been a long while / He see my cowboots

untucked / beats me / a whole   country / mile

/ My skin's / patterned   wilder / than a

oriental   rug / Roll this house up Benny /

she's a fool of jittabugs / O life's table's

tilted hen's / eggs all   quacked / That church

on Wheeling Creek / burn   all / her hymnals

black / cause God's skin / gone   redder 'an

my / skinning board / I've met Paul Luke John / but

not a single Lord   of Lords / How many

prayers / done   come out Lafayette / Holy /

Ghost ain't heard   a single one / done draw

Him down none yet / Well Lord take a peek / now /

your only son's caught   the shakes / Even

after years without fuss / years stealing

break after   break / Serve me / a warm plate of

right blessings / a mountain of hotcakes / Still

nothing   taste quite as good / as one more

clean   clear   slake / Come on

let's put a lid / atop this old / house Benny / Past

ain't worth a thing / but an old wheat penny / Past

ain't worth   a damn thing / but   an old

wheat penny   Past   ain't   worth

a damn thing / but   an old wheat   penny

What You Left Behind in Wheeling, WV

When the sheets are threaded tighter
than the silver trout line of her hair,
you think maybe tonight you could've
skipped grandfather's belt buckle:
its turquoise pebbles leaving quite
an impression, a whole creek bed
cracked across her thighs.

If the bathroom light calls like a lantern,
then you spill drunk across her shore.
Sinking in the echo of her tiny vanity,
maybe you should've sheared
each black hair out the hollows
of your cheeks. But, then would she still call
you *my crow-feathered Injun*?

But you won't linger long in Wheeling, WV
and there's nothing quite like getting used
to a lover with the same name as your grandma.
Before you ever will, she'll die, will-less, leaving
nothing but this girl as inexplicable call back.
In three days, you'll even lose the belt buckle.

"What was his name again?" she asks.
"Hmm," you say, now awake.
"Your Grandad with that belt," she says.
"Lonely Stars," you mumble.
"So romantic," she says.
She asks, "That really his name though?"
"They ain't let him have it long," you say.
She nods her head, as if she gets it.

Rocking, under a creek bed of cracked stars,
you hold her, let yourself linger long—
long as the buckle's impression will last.

A. Real. Uncle. TomTom.

Oh I wish / I was in the land of cotton. / Old times
they are not forgotten. / There's buckwheat cakes
& Injun batter. / Makes you fat or a little fatter.
Look / away! Look away! / Look away! Dixie Land
—20TH CENTURY BLACKFACE MINSTREL SHOW

Dear Koda / Little Brother,

Remember us / fat on battered cans of Miller Light: our bodies browning, slowed
/ by the champagne! of! beers! You reaching / with a clarifying finger toward the
camouflage boy / Shawnee boy / propped up on a cattycorner barstool. You growled
at his shaved head & army-issued rucksack / twisting like Quetzalcoatl's tail around
his boots. You called him / A. Real. Uncle. TomTom. / & I would've / said that was
ingenious / *what a play / on words* / but you weren't ever playing about being Indian.

Shooting / hoop after hoop on a no-net rim / hell / even swinging from cracked
blacktop monkey bars / you'd tell 'em straight those white boys asking, *How Indian*
are you really? / "Us? We're Iroquois as finding corn in your shit / Native as a
thunderbird tattoo," / you proclaimed. / We prayed nightly to the god of the Sioux.
Tadodaho was our great grandfather. / We kept / the council fire / the people's
history. 100 percent / Onondaga & don't doubt it or we'll run / you over with our
canoe. But really

we're polluted / as the Monongahela / Mënaonkihëla / River "where banks cave in
or erode." / That's us / an easy top 10 / on the toxic water index / & eroding. Our
granddaddy's Injun batter whisked into pipeline oil / casseroled in plywood caskets
/ longing for the long rest of family / us young-bodied & too poor to remember the
taste / of tradition. / Forgive us forefathers for we know not what we / 're doing.
You left us like folk song / like the longhouse. *For a better life.* "Down toward Dixie."
But you barely made it / 300 miles / south just past Quemahoning Creek / its steep
banks. / "And aren't we just the drainage," everyone said.

Fall

Barberry bushes have been trampled all day
and some boys along the creek
pretending it is the barbed wire of an Indian prison
lay prone clutching nickel-plated revolvers
imaginary of course. Unlike our Reservations
about choosing the wrong side of this battlefield.
Cowboys gallop red across the stripped horses
of their pink legs embarrassing Indians
into a shirtless whoop of bows and
arrows falling dead BANG BANG
barbs fired from prepubescent lips.
Swimming in the music of a clear October
morning eagles handcuff the sun
bald as our understanding
of war never ending ever was.

Our American Punnett ; Square Now?
Square it.

Wwhite skin   ;   Bblue eyes

For every Male Penobscot Indian
above the Age of Twelve Years,
that shall be taken and brough to Boston,
Fifty Pounds.... For every "

Wwhite skin   ;   Bblue eyes

yyellow river   ;   Rred sky

Penobscot Indian taken and brought
in as aforesaid, and for every Male Indian
Prisoner under the Age of Twelve Years,
taken and brought in as aforesaid, "

BBlack field   ;   **our genocide**

Rred skin   ;   bbrown eyes

SCALP of a Male Penobscot Indian
above the Age aforesaid, brought in
as Evidence of their being killed as aforesaid,
Forty Pounds.... For every Female "

RRed skin   ;   Bbrown eyes

but we are alive   ;   but we are alive

Twenty-five Pounds.... For every SCALP
of such Female Indian or Male Indian
under the Age of Twelve Years,
that shall be killed and brought in "

but we are alive   ;   i am alive

---

n By His Honour, Spencer Phips
Lieutenant-Governor and Commander in Chief,
in and over His Majesty's Province
of the Massachusetts-Bay in New-England
where *the Tribe of Penobscot Indians have repeatedly*
in a perfidious Manner acted contrary
to their solumn Submission unto His Majesty
long since made and frequently renewed

36

—

As Dew, Born / As Dew,

between the frown of a bow & happy bullet

between the age of horse & an iron shoe

between years of plenty & the atomic minute

my ojiisan barters a month

of rice for the brown body of a grand

piano gifted into the beloved

palms of his wife

      would life be   two winters of rice

      or one spring   of music

our family will hear over

how many torn continents

of war.

Born Year of the Uma

Scuffing our sneakers on crumbled
blacktop basketball courts dog-calling
Hialeah-hollering I say, *Is there anything
more than Corey being born
in the year of the faggy horse? Bitchass*
We cackle loud enough to light crows off
telephone poles & of course it's really me
who's ashamed of being horse-born year
after upended year still star sign of the
discolored stallion Me who is faggy
My bitchass

clings saddle-tight & nightly dreams
of my mare She is brown my
mare so brown as turned earth my nude
body blending perfection paint wet
across her bumpy spine ropes of her
dark mane malting against my small
chest I lay awake most nights
her dreaming like me to
crossover the shoals of some fairy-tale
body of river racing muddy through
field of green after
green

But I grow hand over hand sixteen hands
longer than the muscled trunk of her & in the
illness of my youth fading I beg to be reborn
year of the Ox

huffing gold clouds misted in tall grass with
horns long enough to hang the worries of my
small worlds or begat by Tiger years of

cleaning manblood from my claws snagged
dewy through green stalks reaching long as
earth's static hair for the underbelly to remake me
in the image of the great red god of a dragon
the years I prayed to spit fire to sling fangs to
fly far from the black hearth of yet another
abusive boy's home

When finally I dream again of her my
mare she is dead. There is nothing but
a paling body a corpse spilled oilslick
in the dirt So I skin her I quarter her I
pack her tough meat to sell on street
corners Because O I have grown for
so long long look at me & my claws
of the Tiger how I flayed her long like
the horns of the Ox how I speared her
long like the fangs of the red god how
I devoured her Finally ruthless I am
the heart
of a
Dragon
unmade
not long
for oblivion.

Between a Somerset Kitchen and Conodoguinet Creek

for Matsume Hasebe

In spring wind / peach blossoms begin / to come apart. /
Doubts do not / grow branches and / leaves.
-DŌGEN ZENJI, SŌTŌ SCHOOL OF ZEN FOUNDER

Our fishing trip begins with a death
poem written on a napkin, however,
not hastily but urgent blue fountain
pen left on the kitchen table for all
her daughters, but I'm the one
who pocketed it.

>*In spring wind*
>*peach blossoms*
>*begin to come apart.*

How was I to know she could quote
Dōgen? I was seven and still sleepy
but, *The fish don't sleep long*, says obaasan
my little grandmother, Matsume
making me repeat it over and over
until I am bleating: o–*baa*–san—
o–*baa*–san — o–*baa*–san
like a sheep. She strokes the black wool
of my head and says, when I jab
at her with the end of an oar, not
to upset our boat, *He who has been so kind.*
She routs a sixth Marlboro Red, her fifth
still blossoming peach from compressed lips.

>*Doubts do not grow*

Trout flash white over shards of broken
basalt. The creek rolls its shoulders across
the smooth bottom of our kindhearted boat. Rays
are corked yellow behind an Appalachian
foothill. The glossy fractals of our fishhooks
an excuse to tangle lines of communication.
Shocks of light reach low for river face
between

    branches and leaves.

Do you know about death? she says
and with time I nod, thumbing slow over the finale,
the last blue line of her poem in my pocket:

But there will be no spring   for me.

In the Garden, Winter's Cherry

> *The giant*
> *snake's eyes*
>   *are akakagachi,*
> *of one*
>   *body, but*
> *eight heads*
>   *and eight tails.*
>   —THE KOJIKI, URTEXT OF JAPANESE MYTHOLOGY

Akakagachi

as paper lantern

    as the cut bellies

of eight winter

    cherries

are my father's eyes

    when he hears

of the giant snake

    in our neighbor's garden

        Shadows

    slither from his heels

        while he makes the walk

    short with shovel

        with knife

with a coiled roll

    of duct tape

The color

has long washed

from my Superman

pajamas yellowing

quicker than

crepuscular twilight

pooling at tiny feet

pissing myself

in true fear

of his arrival

with the snake's

black body

with the snake's

severed head

Wrap it shut,

he says, *or it will*

still bite

My small hands

sticky with silver

tape I peel apart

beneath

the unhinged

jaws of a giant.

Hunting WASPs: Camp Rodney, 2001

*On my honor, I will do my best to do my duty to God and my country
and obey the Scout Law; to help other people at all times; to keep myself
physically strong, mentally awake, and morally straight.*
—THE SCOUT OATH

On my honor
we flared out
around a picnic table
akimbo
so much prepubescent
sweat steeping
our khaki uniforms brown
beneath shocks of blonde sunlight.
We didn't look
like the scouts on the manual
that is to say whiteboys but boy
could we ever tie up
our neckerchiefs in a knot.
We didn't have the right
badges but there was
no shortage of flagpoles
to wind up as baseball bats.
We smashed can
after can after can
of emerald Mountain
Dew shaken up until the picnic
table awash in globs of green
syrup and sparkling sunshine
all of us leaning in to see
a handful of wasps
plastered to tabletop
pinned beneath the weight
of brilliant dollops
hissing carbonation. There

we squatted above wood planks
greedy with our picnic.
We relished
the knowledge of wet wings
mired beneath our boots
dumb to the methods of mercy
able only to imagine
their greatest agony.

On the Occasion I Participated in Two Very Different Flag Burnings

2000.
We called it *retiring*
Old Glory, Troop 276,
us middle school boys
in our green 'n tans
uniforms filling every concrete crease
of a United Methodist church's
parking lot. "Under the code,"
said the Scoutmaster, "the flag,
when it is in such condition
that it is no longer a fitting symbol
for display, should be obliterated.
By burning."
He turned to us boys with bent arms
held at weakest attention. 640
flags cast carefully over
the long iron teeth of a smoldering pit,
soft names muffled beneath the black girth
of its tongue. Fire filled our eyes,
flags dissolving like ice.

2020.
Them and Us.
Blue and Brown.
Batons and bedsheets burning red, white, &
we are scattering
in the face of weaponized Blue.
Some of us are free
to wonder about speech.
Others tongue-tossed, tied in metal infinity
symbols. Names chanted. Protestor's lips:
Jordan Edwards. Jayson Negron. Terence Crutcher. Breonna Taylor. Atatiana Jefferson. Aura R Paul Casi
Our teeth are stained from talking of the deep black,
of insatiable fire pits. We wave red tongues

above the face of a tyrant, our only
recourse the soft lash of symbolic gesture.
In the parking lot, they greet us with an older glory:
with rubber bullets, with sandbags, with helmets and shields,
with enough tear gas and muzzle fire to fill our eyes,
flags dissolving in the wake of ICE.

When your father is barely literate enough to read from the Bible aloud, but you so love there is even this one moment he will share with you

And the Lord said, "What have you done?
The voice of your brother's blood
is crying to me from the ground.
       —GENESIS 4:10

Why   *didn't God*

accept Cain's   *sacrifice*

I ask   my Paw

wisps of white hair   antlers

branching   from the crown

of his head   *Because*

sure as   *shit* Paw said

God ain't   *no vegetarian.*

on first memories   two

i couldn't have been   three
because by then we'd moved 'a new

trailer always groaning legs   would get
out from under them woods

where my Father's jacketed wing is   a whip
for clay birds their discus a fractal of orange

i sit nearby on a stump and grasp   here
where He pulls the brightness from sound

the fall of   timbre
gunfire

teaching my daughter Japanese: 軍 in a single syllable, America

after there were more mass shootings than days in 2019

Gun   is army   in Japan

even one   gun   is *Army*

in America

America Our Punnett ; *SCALP of a Male Penobscot Indian brought in as Evidence*
Square Now ; *of their being killed as aforesaid, Forty Pounds every Female*
Square It ; *under the Age of Twelve Years, that shall be killed and brought in* [n]

Wwhite skin ; Bblue eyes   Wwhite skin ; Bblue eyes

Rred skin ; bbrown eyes   RRed skin ; Bbrown eyes

yyellow river ; Rred sky   Black field ; genocide

they were alive ; i am alive   they were alive ; i am alive

---

n By His Honour, Spencer Phips
Lieutenant-Governor and Commander in Chief,
in and over His Majesty's Province
of the Massachusetts-Bay in New-England
where *the Tribe of Penobscot Indians have repeatedly*
in a perfidious Manner acted contrary
to their solumn Submission unto His Majesty
long since made and frequently renewed

just another flying   river haiku

red   the salmon balks

      a blue breath true   what leaps

cannot   change its flow.

red   the salmon balks

a blue breath *true*   *what leaps*

cannot   change its flow?

54

Son of a Klansmen's Daughter

Dear Uncle,

I heard you couldn't bear
witness to a black woman
climbing the ladder
of opportunity that was
one of your twenty-six peach trees,
so you *cut*
every last one of them fuckers
down with a chainsaw
—blade *right at the base.*

Dusted 'em all
—ten minutes flat, ha!

Hard,
I thought about equivalences
for hate: maybe seeds,
old trees, or an unyielding
stump—the roots
of a nurtured sprout,
how strong the need
for water—a steady source,
how strong the need
for a kindness
of sun.

Maybe
you are fragile,
a decanter's mouth dripped
into—decades of gardeners
passing until you became
a man, full
of a kind of seed,

of a kind of watering,
of a kind of fruit.

I want to ask
if you ever loved
that razed orchard—
but of course
we haven't spoken
since I was just a sprout,
raised and watered beneath
orchard branches, then
budding with peach fuzz—
here, I see myself—again,
again I press
a different tine, another kind
of blade. Deep
into my body, I search
right at the base, I root
for a different kind
of seed,
of tree,
of fruit—
my mouth longing
for the flavor
of fresh water.

Quiescence

Youtube:
phones heard
infiltrate

Pulse Nightclub:

2:05 A.M. on E.

Of the same

eddied syllabic

light.

so much

dancefloor-dimmed

this the point) about

ringing

without.

phone

phone

chorus of unanswer

ring. A single floor lit

Amongst Chaos

a dozen abandoned
ringing as police
Pulse Nightclub

Of the same

Baltimore 2019

Saratoga St.

Name and Tongue and Breath

exchange dangling

This night after

Salt and Heat and Noise

we forget (and wasn't

the endless

those bodies

Each well-armored

after

begging. This thin

after tones. The ever

with loved ones

calling for

                               ever

against the silence

                               of an empty

dancehall.

Punnett ; America [11]

	WWhite skin ;	BBlue eyes
BBlue eyes	RRed skin ; BBrown eyes BBlue river ; CClear sky	Rred skin ; Bbrown eyes Bblue river ; Cclear sky
; WWhite skin	rred skin ; bbrown eyes bblue river ; cclear sky	light skin ; heavy eyes yellow river ; red sky black field ; our genocide but we are alive ; I am alive

just another love   bird poem

when

     i was   seven

we   had a bird

     cage   with seven

bent   arms

     & seven   times

i   would walk

     around

my two tiny   lovebirds

     whistling

as   if i was

     conductor

of the   kitchen

     their   watermelon

bodies   seeding seven colors

     of happiness

like   sherbet

     like   fresh fruit

laid out by   my mother

     Love always   *needs*

two   she said

You   are my

number two   then

        one   lovebird

laid seven   soft

        white eggs   & when

her mate   stooped

        into   the nest

to get a better   look

        she   opened

the   back

        of his green   skull

seven times her   beak

        pecking &   pecking

the   splintering

                bone

his   pulp

        ringing

her   beak

        so much   darker

than the   fruit

        of their two   small

bodies   unslung.

just another friday night   drug poem

four skeletons stretch hatted   around a bonfire

bundled bones   teeth spent charcoal cluster

scullery white of ribcage and open   eyed all of them

here is the red of every   fuck

daggered tooth   and clawing cloak

but here is this beat   beat of four friends

red hearts furnace   dripped

molten   and still with every possibility

small talk or in my hand   galaxies

it looks like the thief rocketed
their whole self through
the bull's eye of my driver's side door
and you're not wrong to expect
the old joke about there being
nothing in my car worth the thieving
or maybe i've caught you eyerolling
please god not another
poem about windows but i cross my
fingers hope to die suck on diesel
and be hogtied i'll avoid simile
for the eye and soul and i'll be
careful as the fixer's hands
who came to pry waterlogged
lining from my inner door
her small boots crunching sun in the
glittered puddle of fractured glass
i think how i didn't think to sweep
but even so she is still kind i think
to get her a glass of tap water now
but then think of all the stairs
she says this big sol reminds her
of cuba y tu she asks but i don't
relish speaking spanish anymore
i tell her no i have always lived
here in miami i lie but offer my father
was a mason and bueno too at that
i've given her this one fractled truth as if
it could be understood not to mistake
my soft handshake for ignorance
of all the working classes but she
is not thinking of me only the door's
motor grinding she asks but what do i do
i hope she will ask

if maybe i am a mason myself but no
i say i am maybe a writer
me too she beams and offers a full palm
of what she'd vacuumed from the doorframe
shattered glass beads of blue refraction
wonder she says wonder at all they have
seen she insists ver toward the tiny eyelets
en mi mano galaxias she says and i wonder
how often i have mistaken myself
for the seer for the see-er
and others simply as the seen.

The Face of a Man

"Ain't such a thing
        as a lynx
—not even bobcat
        kin out here in East Jesus,
PA," says Tommy Rico.

Quarrel smokes
        above our fire pit,
and the Old One's lawn chair
        sinks another half inch
into muck and gravel
        clods. "My father told
of a wandering
        lynx," he says, "And now...
we have all seen
        the end of its wandering."

True, we had all heard
        and maybe even seen,
but it's me wandering
        down into this gully—
dawn's placenta dribbling,
        runny over Kittatinny
mountain heads—
        me and my
little fingers
        clutching a wide-mouthed
pail of gasoline.

My nostrils plugged
        with cotton,
my lips light pink
        beneath black
Harley-Davidson bandanna,

six matches
lined in the elastic band
      of my favorite underwear.
All it should take,
      they'd said.

"The lynx spirit
      cannot wound the pure
heart of a boy,"
      they'd agreed.
And again, I was offered up,
      sacrificed,
on the altar
      of my father's pride.

I splay out
      my legs, hairless—and careful
not to disturb even a shrub
      sloping—into a hollow
of the creek's left nostril.
      My sneakers slide
across constellations
      of dew shimmer,
sometimes tangled
      in thickets of hairy earth.
I look up
      from careful footing
and offer my chin
      against lobes of purpling light.

Dawn outlines the lithe
      silhouette of a man belly
down, unnatural,
      as if he'd come
exhausted from between
      hips of the creek's feeble

current—shore side
       he lies chin propped
upon a stone,
       as if he would sip at
one more cup of air,
       as if he would face
the eyes of his unmaker.

A billion gnats discuss
       who will suck the sweat
out the cheesecloth
       of my white tee.
Even the peach fuzz
       of my small belly stands
straight with fear.

But I slosh the gasoline.
       I ladle the whisper of match glow.
I wonder if he will
       speak to me:
the voice of an old god
       beneath the work of my hands.

just another   window poem

a banquet hall   gyred beat this bonfire
scrapes   winter's ceiling

a small bird   outside
lept windowsill   of all taxonomy
flutters   inside
doved one open   window

she searches   for warmth
now the briefest   of flight

flies   out again through another

so is life   says my abuelita
so is life   says my obaasan
in the banquet hall   of all dying

who can ask   this bird
before   after
life's two   open windows

For my daughter who loves spiders & beetles & black nail polish

for those who hear the glacier's heartbeat
led by the moon with both eyes closed
what trees toss away their branches
& refuse the slipping back into any outline
of their old self yet tug the braid of all creation
these embers that gleam beneath the ash
between the simmer of soup & kettle hiss
where a small girl discovers the Atlas of Heaven
there's gold here & there's fools gold too
so spin.

Final Paean of the Dowser

Search not for water,
but the briny surfaces
of my inner most parts:
blistered cities, a damnable
penchant for dark corners.
I'll agree to rewrapped psalms,
begrudgingly, biblical in new
butcher paper, just give me
the E.M.R. straight (by doctor's
orders, no chasers). Am I, too, old
to bang the heart's gong over
this spilled meat: what is left?
of these last days.

n

	WW ; BB
WW ; BB	ReSk ; BrEy
	ReSk ; live

Benjamín Naka-Hasebe Kingsley belongs to the Onondaga Nation of Indigenous Americans in New York. He is the author of *Dēmos*, *Colonize Me*, and *Not Your Mama's Melting Pot*, winners and finalists of over a dozen awards. Affrilachian poet and Kundiman alum, Naka-Hasebe Kingsley is recipient of the Provincetown Fine Arts Work Center and Tickner Fellowships. His work has appeared in numerous publications such as *The BreakBeat Poets: LatiNEXT*, *Native Voices: Honoring Indigenous Poetry*, *The Georgia Review*, *Kenyon Review*, *Oxford American*, *Poetry*, & *Tin House*. He is an assistant professor of poetry and nonfiction in Old Dominion University's MFA program.

milkweed
editions

Founded as a nonprofit organization in 1980, Milkweed Editions is an independent publisher. Our mission is to identify, nurture and publish transformative literature, and build an engaged community around it.

Milkweed Editions is based in Bde Ota (Minneapolis) within Mni Sota Makoče, the traditional homeland of the Dakota people. Residing here since time immemorial, Dakota people still call Mni Sota Makoče home, with four federally recognized Dakota nations and many more Dakota people residing in what is now the state of Minnesota. Due to continued legacies of colonization, genocide, and forced removal, generations of Dakota people remain disenfranchised from their traditional homeland. Presently, Mni Sota Makoče has become a refuge and home for many Indigenous nations and peoples, including seven federally recognized Ojibwe nations. We humbly encourage readers to reflect upon the historical legacies held in the lands they occupy.

milkweed.org

Interior design by Mary Austin Speaker & Tijqua Daiker
Typeset in Caslon by Tijqua Daiker

Adobe Caslon Pro was created by Carol Twombly
for Adobe Systems in 1990. Her design was inspired by
the family of typefaces cut by the celebrated engraver
William Caslon I, whose family foundry served
England with clean, elegant type from the early
Enlightenment through the turn of the
twentieth century.